The Split Pomegranate

The Split Pomegranate
© 2025 Melineh Ani Yemenidjian
ISBN:9781966337171

Cover art
© 2025, Norayr Yemenidjian

Author Photo
© 2025, D. Hideo Maruyama

First Edition, 2025

Printed in the United States of America

Edited by Ghislaine LeFranc
Cover Design by Shiva Nosrati
Layout Design by Ensieh Lali

DAXSON
PUBLISHING

This book is a labor of love, just like raising my two boys, Norayr and John. I leave this book as a legacy to them. May they have the freedom to explore their lives in a way that sparks meaning and purpose.

Praise for *The Split Pomegrante*:

"…where many debut collections remain in the realm of confession, Melineh transcends. What sets her apart is the way she tempers urgency with precision, shaping a collection that is both luminous and devastating, carried by a stunning arc of reckoning and revelation."

—Shahé Mankerian, *History of Forgetfulness*

"*The Split Pomegranate*, Melineh's first poetry collection, is both raw and exquisitely crafted, brimming with depth and richness. Through her deft command of language, she transforms pivotal moments from her life into an authentic, emotional journey through life-altering experiences. Her vivid imagery and precise expression seamlessly weave together her inner and outer worlds."

—Talar Keoseyan, *The Armenian Weekly*

"*The Split Pomegranate* is a ceremony of survival—a 'scar carved on Beauty,' cells of undetonated grief, coffee boiling in a New Jersey kitchen. Melineh Ani Yemenidjian refuses resolution, offering persistence instead: 'Poems are scavenged tombs that can never / again be sealed.' Here, the personal and ancestral blur, as grief, memory, and witness move together, carrying 'iris of sky' and 'horse shoes were beaten / into the soles' toward an unquiet truth. Let us welcome Yemenidjian, struck with the complexities of being human, to the literary world where she belongs."

— Arthur Kayzakian, *The Book of Redacted Paintings*

"Although gloriously steeped in Armenian American culture, this collection reflects the experiences of all women with precise clarity, as well as deep feeling, from girlhood to wiser and sharper womanhood. It is a treat in precise, frank language and imagery that you can sink into and think, 'Yeah! She just went there. Good for her.' An experience not to be missed."

—Lisa Montagne, Ed.D., professor and author of *Robot Lover*

"*The Split Pomegranate* is a winding road through struggles with depression and finding light through poetry. Yemenidjian does not sugar coat any of the peaks and valleys that bleed on these pages. 'Poems are the beat that drives us all.' The pace of her prose becomes the rapid thump in your chest. This journey will make you smile and also wipe a few tears. What I enjoy about Yemenidjian's poetry is the well-crafted details. She chisels similes on the page like an expert sculptor. Nathaniel Hawthorne said, 'Easy reading is damn hard writing.' This is hard writing with a nice balance of complexity that will leave the reader satisfied like enjoying a strong cup of coffee boiled three times."

—Tommy Domino, *Closer in the Rearview* and *Switches, Hot Wheel Tracks, and Extension Cords*

The Split Pomegranate

A Memoir in Poetry

Melineh Ani Yemenidjian

«Նուռը կկիսես, հազար մտածում կը գայ:»

"When you split open a pomegranate,
countless thoughts and ideas come to mind."

—Armenian Proverb

Table of Contents

II.

III.

IV.

Foreword

This is written for the love of my life that I have the privilege of calling "my ole' lady."

There are moments in life that define us—fragments of joy, sorrow, love, and loss that shape who we become. For better or worse, my wife has wholly experienced those moments, and in this collection, she lays them bare with a rare honesty that only poetry can communicate.

These pages are not just words; they are glimpses into the depths of her spirit and soul. For in this collection, she walks the fragile line between shadow and light, tracing the contours of her mind like a trembling hand over worn pages. The storms within her have names she now speaks aloud, no longer a whisper, no longer a weight she bears alone. In acceptance, there is release—in understanding, a transformative strength that carries her forward.

I have had the privilege of witnessing her journey—through triumphs and heartbreaks, through days of light and nights of doubt. And now, she offers that journey to you, unfiltered and unguarded. It is both a gift and a challenge: to see, to feel, and to understand the life behind these lines.

I invite you to step into Melineh's poems with an open heart. They are the story of a woman who has loved fiercely, endured quietly, and emerged with wisdom that only time and experience can grant. This is her truth. And now, it is yours to carry.

—Christopher Yemenidjian

I.

"I am made and remade continually.
Different people draw different words
from me."

—*Virginia Woolf*

The Split Pomegranate
After a drawing by Norayr Yemenidjian, age 8

The pomegranate is a
collection of dreams,
archived in rows of
brilliant beads,
safely embedded
in a spongy, white
membrane

When cracked open,
its sharp sweetness
travels to the nose
while a rosy river
seeps into my pores

The best part
is to peel back the rind,
and trace the path
branched in two
before sinking teeth
in this fruit,
and thanking
the short season
for its gift

Poems

Poems are splinters excavated by needles

Poems are scavenged tombs that can never
again be sealed

Poems are wasps inside a fig

Poems are underestimating the ocean's strength

Poems are oil leaks a thousand feet deep

Poems are undetonated explosions

Poems are longshots

Poems are coffee rings on a first draft

Poems are red-rimmed eyes and shoulders
dusty with dandruff

Poems are retired men skipping in slippers

Poems are lovers in various states of undress

Poems are lives taking notes on the body

Poems are deaths by a thousand cuts

Poems are mobs bearing buckets of tar and feathers

Poems are warring tribes flooding green hills

Poems are refugees seeking sanctuary

Poems are waking up

Poems are frogs resting by a lotus on a water lily

Poems are echoes of silence

Poems are the beat that drive us all

Jeweler's Daughter
After "Baker's Son" by Shahé Mankerian

I.

Baba is a
good man. He
takes off his shoes
in the closet
after work.

Mama, luminous
like the candle
she lit for him
the first time
they met,

Welcomes
him, wearing a skirt—
I tell them to get
a room.

He pads down the hall.

Upon returning,
he smells of
the garden in
Mama's dreams.

Before dinner,
while he plays
the guitar,
Baba reads the
circle of fifths
like the Bible.

I close my eyes
and listen to
his prayers.

His fingertips
pluck notes of
family, and the
rests are tremors
of silent memories.

II.

When Baba's pinky links
with mine during *shoorch
bar,** he is a child again—

He remembers the craters
landscaping summer—
oranges picked near
the Mediterranean Sea

Instead of running
away from the bomb that
landed on his neighbor's
building in Beirut.

He no longer has to spend
his steps looking for shelter
in rubble, because he is safe in
this circle moved by music.

III.

I have eyes
like Baba's
old soul.

They are
the night sky,
balancing
a perfect
planet.

Then a blazing
dawn rising from
the stirring
ocean.

When he sits
next to me
cupping tea—

I know he
is at ease.

IV.

His eye pressed
against a loupe,
Baba inspects
an engagement
ring.

He has just set
the center stone
in four prongs—
2.5 carats and
nearly flawless.

When I see
his cracked
and blackened
fingers,

Pinching
this fragile
sliver, I think of
when his hands
were once empty.

Then I feel
forlorn—
like diamond
dust.

Yet, it does not settle,
for it flows between us—

Until
we eat
cake.

Shoorch bar (Շուրջ պար) is a traditional Armenian circle dance.

Childhood

Original text from "A Woman of the World: The Dancer of Shamakha" by Armen Ohanian used for transformative artistic purposes*

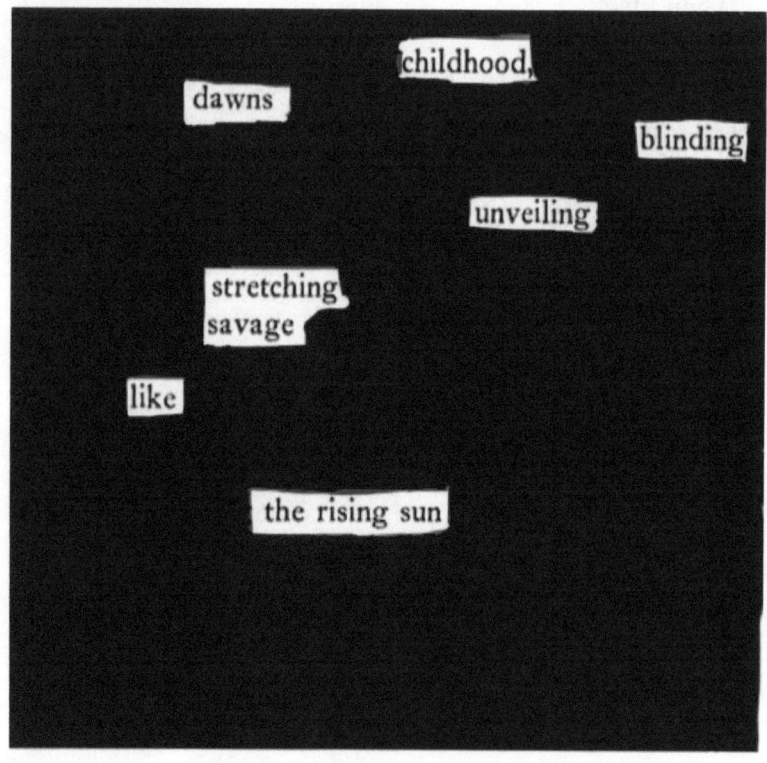

*All black out poems in this book are from this source.

Harbinger

I witnessed the emergence
of a dove from an egg—
smooth and white, like a pearl

Fallen from the eave
of my roof after strong winds
tore the nest asunder

Its mother had flown on
to build her home in a safer place—
leaving her unborn hatchling
to fend for itself

Featherless and hungry,
through hazy eyes,
it is not wretched,
but part of nature's order

Religion at Armenian School
Santa Ana, California, 1996

The sun filtered
through stained glass
and cast a veil
on Der Hayr's bearded face—
his eyes flashed,
then turned to flint

Incense burned our nostrils
and monotone sermons
of Evil Satan, Enemy Turks,
and Tricky Jews bored us

Crammed on wooden pews,
we played hand-games, usually
Down by the Banks
or Double-Double-This-This

He jabbed a finger
in the air
and warned
that his holy dove
spied at our window
and reported wrongdoings
directly to God

Der Hayr was scheduled
to teach our class
every Thursday

Once, he made us
color the crucifix
and chided
if we drew outside
the lines

Tempted to scribble
cerulean on Jesus's face,
I feared God's wrath
and neatly outlined
the cross in brown

i can't help myself, i'm a 90s kid

shenanigans are
six friends in my living room
shifting to third gear

Tripp Circle

My little sister, Anoush
spins in the plastic pool—
her curly hair sticks to her
face as she twirls and plops

We have a silver swing set
with a metal slide; heated by
the sun, inch by inch, it
burns our poor behinds

Nene, in her floral dress,
picks grape leaves off the vine—
her *sarma** is the best,
made with love right inside

Baba sits on a folding chair
playing *Sari Siroon Yar*,
smiling with his crinkled eyes,
and strumming the guitar

Mama carries watermelon
and braided Armenian cheese;
a camera swings on her wrist
to capture all she sees

I am found writing poems,
cross-legged on the grass,
dreaming away the bully that
had tortured me in class

Sarma is a traditional Armenian dish of stuffed grape leaves—
usually with rice and spiced ground beef, but for my family, it was
always vegetarian.

Sari Siroon Yar (Սարի Սիրուն Եար) is an Armenian folk song. It
translates to "Beautiful Beloved of the Mountain).

As a Flower Girl at My Aunt's Wedding
Boston, Massachusetts, 1996

I cried at your wedding as I felt overlooked—
with so many grown-ups looming about
it's easy to feel lost at eight years old,
when no one cares to hear me shout

You remind me when you visit,
that I stained the day—by folding my arms,
pinching my face, and refusing to speak
because they all ignored my charms

As the firstborn, I was conditioned
to be praised and taught to perform—
it was the only time adults would listen
to a child, restless and torn

When a tide of emotion rolls in
that children can't express—
it is perceived as ill behavior
instead of a need to be addressed

So, when you point your finger
even in the spirit of jest,
it jabs the little girl inside me—
like I'm still a stubborn pest

The Undying Goodbye

To my mother, Maggie—
the eternal Elvis fan
Philadelphia, Pennsylvania, 1977
After "Love Me Tender" by Elvis Presley

She was only sweet fifteen
When she heard the news
It said Elvis met defeat
No one could rejoice

This isn't true, bring him back!
Tears fell down her face
Her whole world has turned to black
He can't be replaced

She was only sweet fifteen
And she had no choice
She, a queen, had lost her king
Her cries were just noise

Let me watch! Only this once
He is worth my life
I will run away for months
I could have been his wife

Elvis still lives on the stage
She built in her mind
Here, she is free from the cage
That was left behind

Dance with me, sing with me
Spread your golden wings
We will shine forever more
Despite everything

Night Love

The midnight sky, silent and deep
Has two solitary stars in its keep
Shining bright like my two eyes
Watching over you through the days
  going by

As you sleep warm in your bed
My stars descend and kiss your head
Though we are separated, our hearts
  far
The closeness we feel it will not mar

Through the night our hearts sing
  strong
It will be morning not before long
When finally we will get to dance
The rising sun will give us that chance

At last, the sun has come out bright
Its warm rays hold us tight
Another day still contains hope
If not, we will still cope

If more days pass by, that we do not
  see eye to eye
We will still be under the same night
  sky

Poem by Melineh Merdjanian

Heedless

Tread on a threat
like it is a pebble
though it sticks
to your sole

The butterfly dances
until it is pinned
because beauty is
mummified gossamer

Serial killer
pseudo thriller
viral virus
like hepatitis

We are hungry
among amber waves
the sun is not enough
for photosynthesis

Children do not chase
glowing fireflies
instead they are dumped
in two dimension

Vista point
off the freeway
unattainable
sacrosanct

When You Don't Want to Fuck
Costa Mesa, California, 2004

You slipped away from your friends
to meet him at the county fair
for the first time

You passed the pungent smell
of manure, then popcorn and heard
country twang line dancing off the stage

He stood by the entrance, and your body
grew warm because in real life,
he looked just as cute

But instead of leading him
to the hay-strewed ground, he
navigated you toward the pavement,

then urged you to climb in the
back of his car. It was small and
littered with empty fast food
wrappers and dirty clothes

Your brain froze,
just like the screen
when the dial-up
internet goes down

He pulled your waist close—
his crushed kiss tasted
like an old shoe

Then he laid you until
your head knocked against
the closed window

His body descended and
swallowed yours whole

So that no one could
hear you scream

After, he zipped
his pants and lit a
cigarette while your
bra remained clutched
in your firsts

He took a look at a crumpled
paper bag stained with ketchup
and said, "I'm hungry"

As if you were Ask Jeeves,
and he'd typed in
"how to satisfy a craving,"
you offered,
"How about McDonald's?"

Seventeen
Notepad Confessional*

I was late for seven days—
and for every day, I wore my
black Girl's League sweatshirt
with the hoodie up. My stomach,
hard like a red apple...

*I have kept an ongoing note on my phone that I use to write down
general musings as they happen. These confessionals are a way for
me to mine those spur-of-the-moment gems that I caught in their
moment of resonance.

Aggregation

Questions fill our worried minds
Setting us on top of mines
We try so hard, all the time
To rid the body of this grime
Feeling so guilty of crime
Exhausted by our day's grind
The shards we break off will one
Arduous day intertwine

How to Trap a Butterfly

"It's simple," he said to his son.
"Just pinch your fingers like this."

He brought together index and thumb
over the filmy velvet
of the monarch's wing.

"Will it hurt her?" the boy asked.

"No, she won't feel a thing.
And once we have her,
we can put her in a jar to keep."

"Will she have air?" asked the boy
lifting his face to his father,
eyes wide.

"Of course,
we will poke holes."

"Holes," repeated the boy.

"Quickly," said the father.
"Open the jar so we can put her in."

The son gingerly put his palm
over the lid of the marmalade jar
to twist it open.

It made a sound like a wet kiss.

The father dropped the butterfly
into its translucent chamber
and told the boy to screw
the lid on tightly, and he did.

Father and son watched the butterfly—
wings lost in a flurry of flame.

Without Bounds
Long Beach, California, 2009

The Japanese Garden at
CSULB is my oasis

I delight in how the bridge
curves over the koi pond,
allowing me to explore
just a bit further

Between classes, I walk
across campus and imagine
building a little home
above the waterfall

With no one there,
I sleep under a
cherry blossom tree
and dream about
teaching poetry

Then my phone rings—
it's my fiancée

"Where are you?"

His disdain, a punch
to the gut

"Who are you with?
Is it your lab partner,
that guy?"

"I hope you're not
wearing that skirt
you showed me
this morning."

My face turns red,
my knuckles, white

...but the breeze is so sweet

Without a word
I hang up,
and lift my chin
toward the sun

Rupture

Sometimes good
                    is a soda can
            tossed out a window
        or an eyelash   flicked
            from the tip of a finger.

Thoughts tumble
                    the way Alice
            flips
head to toe down the
                    hole,
        passing shelves lined with
                        nonsense maps
            and books with blank pages.

There is no way to undo
                    carving "I hate you"
on a wall, unless
            it is sanded and painted over.
Yet who would return
                to the scene
        of the crime?

No one can see
        the spotlight shining
    on mental monologues
                that sacrifice similarities
        for a sense of superiority:

This sand can only be flung
                    against the wind,
        to invade the mouth
                    and whither the tongue.

Gross
Notepad Confessional

Unpacking life is
ringing out
snot and tears
from a tissue
and putting it
back into the box

Bitter Grounds
New Jersey, 2010

"You have to let the coffee boil three times, that's how you know it's done," he told me as I stood in front of the stove in his one-bedroom New Jersey apartment. The building looked like a prison, gray and cold. I felt sad there, even though we were in love. He wanted me, at 21 years old, to have his babies and get married in this massive banquet hall near his house. He'd even sent me pictures of the church, all before a marriage proposal.

My grandmother first taught me to make Armenian coffee because it was the duty of a good Armenian woman. Later, he taught me *his* way and it stuck—equal parts finely ground, dark roast coffee and water in the jezve— combine when the water is hot, then boil three times, stirring after every eruption of the foaming liquid. Be careful not to let the coffee overflow onto the stove, otherwise you're left cleaning a mess.

I was making coffee for him and his roommate who played the synthesizer in his band when he sang at weddings, restaurants, and other events. The roommate and his wife stayed in the bedroom while his bed stood behind a wall in the living room. That is where we slept during my stay. That is where we had sex—or tried to.

I held the long handle of the jezve and tilted my wrist slightly so as to not spill a drop—everything had to be perfect. I poured the coffee into small espresso cups with their simple design of green stripes just below the lip. The saucers shook as I walked slowly to the coffee table.

We drank the coffee. I stayed quiet to keep from saying the wrong thing. I had a habit of doing that around him. He had an image to uphold—he wanted me to look and speak like an Arabian princess.

The night before, we had gone to a gig of his at Sayat Nova restaurant. He got really drunk, then ignored me. During the car ride home, I felt discarded and threw a piece of my mind at him.

He stopped the car and said, "I don't care who you are, if you ever talk to me like that again, I will kick you out of this fucking car." Then, all at once, he shoved my arm playfully and laughed.

Later, in bed, he wanted to be intimate, but when he kissed me, his stale cologne and the combination of garlic and whiskey on his breath turned my stomach. He said, "C'mon, you were so good at this before." I acquiesced to avoid disappointment.

After, I turned away to keep him from reading the sediment pooling in my eyes.

Chasm

Cracks on a sidewalk—
valleys;
jumping over
a sheer drop

A chipped shoulder—
broken heart;

Tectonic grind,
fault lines

Your lips move—
the earth quakes

Concealed, 1970

I hid
    my mouth
        in my apron
            when

                he pressed
              the glowing ember
             of his cigarette
         on our daughter's tongue
        forcing her to swallow it
            like medicine

I took
    sheets down
        from the balcony

        as he played house

           with our oldest
           and made her
           the mommy

I dug
    the flesh
        from an eggplant

           while another child
           escaped through me
           like tomato juice
           through a sieve

I cleaned
        dinner
            off the floor

                because his fist hurtled,
                down on the plate
                shattering salvation

The Hole

Today I will make
beans, rice, and chicken.
I will set the table.
The children will come
and the husband will come.
I will sit where I have always
sat, to the left of my husband
who is at the head.

Today I will burn the beans.
He will be mad.
He will slam his hand
flat down on the silverware
that will clink together.

The table will rattle.
It will turn into a hole
deep and black.

In will go
the beans, rice, and chicken;
in the chairs, the table, the children;
in he will go.

I will stand at the mouth
of the splintering abyss
and watch their fingers
grasp at nothing.

I will get the old hoover,
suck up the hole,
grab a beer,
sit down,
and watch TV.

Iridescence

She sits alone
in her dark kitchen,
a plate of stale rye
before her,
waiting for him
to patch the roof
against rain

She stands alone,
iris of sky, while
clouds tremble
with the wrath
of petulant gods; but
it will be she whose
smile will rainbow
across the sky

She saunters alone
as dew twinkles
in her hair, and

With each step
hope sticks
like jacaranda blooms
to the bottom of her soles

Triumph

The whitest sheets
The cleanest feet
Respect to elders
The slimmest shoulders
Resist all sin
Hold it in
Beat the carpet
Be the carpet
Be a lady
Have a baby
Marry young
Innocence strung
He is so old
Hide the gold
Live with his mother
Cherish another
Keep children fed
Dread marriage bed
Swollen once more
Fall to the floor
The floor turns red
Better off dead
God has a plan
Leave that man
His is not reality
Follow family
Seek amnesty
To safekeep daughters
From guilty fathers
And see clearer
In the mirror

Red Wheelbarrow
After William Carlos Williams

Red wheelbarrow
with a belly full
of flowers

It makes me sad
that your wheels
don't move
on their own

I wonder where
you would go
if they did

May I push you

I want to feel
your sturdy handles
against my palms

Please give me
the gift of a splinter
so I may know how it feels
to carry earth

Tea

In Japan they say
you were born
            from eyelids
too tired to stay open—
that you were   ripped out
from a monk's face
  intent on   meditation.
He dropped a seed
                        to the ground
and then you sprouted
      soft green leaves
      and fragrant white petals
encasing
          a tuft of   gold.
With every sip,
you (mystical brew) tingle
my taste buds
      and waft
              the aroma of
serenity   that,
when inhaled, brings hope—
hope of staying awake
long enough to finish
                        a cup,
  long enough
          to live
through the sometimes
          green, white, red, and black
waves
                        of being,

nothing   more
                    (because
nothing
is)
as complex or simple
as a   cup
of
    tea.

Paris
July 2011

Loneliness sat next to me
    inside a cafe's used book store.
          he and i shared a whole quiche
          and stared at a man
          writing a script
        while wearing a scarf
    during summertime.

Loneliness walked with me in le marais
         as we passed
    a surreal mural,
          and a single dead fish
               on the sidewalk.

when i went off to find
        my truth
    from mona lisa's mystical mouth,
      she only mirrored the life
i had left behind.

i indulged Romance—
on pont de arcs
   (above the seine
        where lovers left
locks of devotion)
        then idled, until
   Loneliness sunk my hope
      with tunes from his sad violin.

Solace beckoned me to the moulin rouge—
that bohemian house
  scented with past courtesans
         i desired their trademark beauty—
     nevertheless, their lithe undulations

flicked like a flame i could not touch
        for my fingers still pulsed from Temptation.

i tore away and
                lost myself
        in the crowd
                that swarmed toward
l'arc de triomphe, then scrambled
                from the tourists—for i
                        am an adventurer.

Loneliness found me again
        sitting on a wicker chair
                at a restaurant in les invalides—
                                        sighing
                i lifted the fork to my mouth
                ... and then

                Paris winked at me!
                                she shined
                                through the glass,
                        in front of the
                        eiffel tower
                        and tousled my hair
                with the wind

she took my hand, and
                        led me
                        down
        to le procope
                on rue de l'ancienne comédie where
we spent hours writing and
                        sipping espresso
        with franklin and hemingway

Paris twirled with me
on boulevard saint-germain during a
happenchance
concert
where the streetlamps
bathed us
in orange glow

we drank wine bought from nicholas*
straight
from the bottle

then,
arms over shoulders,
climbed
to l'appartement,
curled against each other
and laughed until
we fell asleep

*A wine retailer in Paris established in 1822.

Drive
Notepad Confessional

                    Ignite your
            headlight* eyes,
to hug
        *winding road
up mountain,
            where midnight*
hangs low,
            and constellations*
wink
        like *friends

Grounded
*Ransom Poem**

YOU BELONG
With Wild
often

A MILE
FROM
Up,

THE
tale
In
your
SMILE

*A ransom poem is a literary concept that combines words and
phrases from magazines and newspapers to create poetry.

Mamihlapinatapei

Fountain Valley, California, July 2011

"The wordless yet meaningful look shared by two
people who both desire to initiate something but
are both reluctant to start."
—From Yagán, the Indigenous language of
Tierra del Fuego

We are naked
as mirrors
that have been
shattered
and put back
together

I see shards
of myself
 in you

Yet, on your side,
it is cold, and fog
mists your glasses

but from where I sit,
cross-legged
in the glistening dust

I see the start of us

under trees, in
the park, eating
watermelon

Bedlam
Ransom Poem

The cracked side of fame/
Perfectly unclear—
Choosing the
American dream!
A scruffy
ensemble
and spirit...
}Illogical and irrational by design{
[An urgent barrier]

47

Fool Me Once

Adonis, a sweet lie
Beloved, a boy whose eyes beguile
Careless the caress of a coward
Downtrodden females dare desire
Ever so lovingly in his arms
Frail turning flower
Glittering guilt
Harmony for the moment
Incandescent, a mirror
Joining one world to the next
Kissing silently in dark alcoves
Laced with lust
Margins melting
Never imagining anything better
Opiate dreams
Perfection contained in a cloud
Queens with alabaster flesh
Regaling in fleeing beauty
Savoring the sweetness of today
Tantamount reality
Undulating like dancing hips
Veering dangerously closer
Weakening the mirage
Xenophobia settling in the bones
Youth and beauty can only be familiar for so long
Zeal and passion fade over time

Mallemuck

To think in terms of opposites
Is to see you in composites.
When I say push, you answer pull—
I can't count rot; it's all just bull.

But to see you is such a heady thrill
That I am already
Infatuated is disaster,
For I cannot wait to fall faster

sunrise during an eclipse
February 2012

just like
your words
that snuff
the shine out
of my eyes,

our tryst is
a candle
turned smoke—
wick charred,
wax pooled,
a reflection
of the moon

shivering
with nothing
to thaw it
but bullets—

embedded
in the softest
part of me—
in the hardest
part of you

Seascape

Molded by the wind—
                    emerging
    unharnessed

The great hull of   sky
rushes
            and dips—
spraying salt
                    like gems

A swell of
            white
    crested wave
                slices through itself

and crashes   on the
                    shore,
                            evermore a beast
                                huffing—

                    its coat shining
                        with sweat

The One Who Cannot Be
Dana Point, California, March 2012

I shouldn't be here—
but I sneak out to be
with the blue-eyed
stranger because he
asked me for the time

I shouldn't be here—
but I ignore mother's
warning for me to stay
away from *odars**

I shouldn't be here—
but he whisks me
to the top of bronzed cliffs
overlooking the harbor
lit by a blanket of sunshine,
then brews my favorite chai
with a portable stovetop

I shouldn't be here—
but that poet-boy
overthrows me
as he strums his guitar
while I sing "Hallelujah"

I shouldn't be here—
but when he leans in
with the horizon in his eyes
and fingers in my hair, I know
here is where I need to be

Odar is the Armenian word for a stranger, or non-Armenian.

That One Time

I was looking for
comfort—you gave
me: raspberries, bree, and
champagne. In the belly of your
houseboat—I felt no fear,
sickness, shame. Your face
said it—all you wanted was to
make me—make you—
make we—rock
with the sea.

fragment

stitching petals
back on a flower

the curling, dried bits
like distressed velvet

a bloom no longer—
now it is art

Replica

Deep wells?
There seem to be none here
only superficial puddles
murky and splattered
on the sidewalk

Stepped in by thousands
clopping to work,
walking the same way
producing the same sounds
day after day

Is there nothing new?
Are my hands just tracing?
Is my voice not working?
Is my heart not speaking?

Today I produced
a replica—
a tired story
of a tired subject

The purpose—
to spill myself out
so you can see inside
of the "tormented writer"
one and the same

Or do I want to be Sylvia Plath?

Carvings in My Journal

What are you?
       Squirming
            into my brain
                 ,   there?

A wriggle
       inside of a cocoon

A few marks to be transformed
            into a flaming
                Monarch?

You are the ear to my
       very loud sky—
       my doomed
            Galaxy;
       my
       Cereal box universe)

So tell me
       how you take it

When I come running
       and scrape you
       with my pen?

When I spill, unintelligibly,
       the Blood
       so willingly
       released?

Do you enjoy being useful
            like this?

Anything to Pass Time—

Anything to pass time—
and please the mind

Emit hate
Teem easel in past
Grit teeth
Lease holes
Mind the mind
Gait guilt
Pass time asleep
Lapse

Please ethos
Ease anything
Get yin and yang
Lute Lush
Sleuth Silence
Hug Nation
Get Lost
Lure Lotus

om

Hours
Ransom Poem

discovery
in
RESTLESSNESS

a
porous
state

BEHIND

challenge

.

On Good Days
Journal Entry, January 13, 2012

Written at The Royal Cup Cafe—
The Definitive Soapbox Open Mic
After Timothy "Big Brother" Cheung

On good days, I call myself a poet. On those days,
my veins fill with ink and I go around bleeding from my
fingertips until the world around me glistens.
On those days, I adore myself, the way I sound, the things I
say, and how I view the world—but only on those days.

I belong to others the rest of the time. I take them
on my shoulders to help unload their burdens. I sleep
with them between their dreams—face pressed
against theirs, radiating warmth, yet bare
without brilliance. Perhaps it's because their bodies
absorb my energy, so I can't tell when I am burnt out.

I need to figure out how to have more good days.

—M.

Wick

Burn low,
      Sweet,
take your

    time.

No life   is
    comparable
  to yours—

    aflame   with
the oil and vinegar
    of gold and blue

which sparks
    the small,
dark room
    that wraps
around skin
      like wax to
          wick.

Let it
    pulse
      and
  drip

    all
      the way
        down

   to cool
      as it pools.

II.

"Sometimes there's a man...
I won't say a hero, 'cause, what's a hero?
But sometimes there's a man—"

—The Big Lebowski

Intuition
Journal Entry

Upon having a conversation with a friend yesterday, I was introduced to a new concept: "Intuition is not inconsistent with logic. In fact, the two feed each other."

He reasoned: "Your intuition is built upon experiences and generalizations of the world. It feels like magic, but it is a mix of you using what knowledge you have already to naturally find your own flow state (which is where things feel magical).

Logic can thus feed more information into intuition, which can be plugged back into logic to further make decisions. They are part of the same system. Automatic responses, such as, learning to block or move without thinking in martial arts, begin as prefrontal neural learning. This eventually becomes "natural instinct" over time and repetition, thus no longer requiring prefrontal "logic circuits." Intuitions are much larger swaths of data, but the consensus is that they work similarly."

This conversation coincided with my recent reading of *The Secret Garden* by Frances Hodgen Burnett which centers on a similar theme. The concept of "magic" in reference to a higher power is central to the book. The higher powers are revealed as strength of mind. If a choice is to live in a storm then stability will not be found—the opposite is just as true: If the mind is clear and calm, new doors will open. To quote *The Secret Garden*, "Two things cannot be in one place. Where you tend a rose, a thistle cannot grow."

Coming alive and merely existing are two different things. This coming year, I will focus on coming alive and enthusiastically meet what is presented before me. The way to do this, I have been told, is through meditation. Preferably in nature. Apparently, in coming alive, I will achieve a "singular calmness."

—M.

Strangerosity

Strangerosity:
A knowing presence of you,
when lost in unknown.

Finding Love, Nevermore
After "The Raven" by Edgar Allen Poe

In my youth, I yearned to marry and did not wish to tarry
by courting men with hungry eyes purchased from an
online store. While I laughed to keep from crying at the
options I was swiping, blinked a message on my cell
phone that shook me to my very core. This must be a
scam, I grumbled; though compelled to know more.
      "Fine, five seconds and nothing more."

I could never vanish that night Aphrodite rendered
as my hope reduced to ember, I felt like faling to the floor.
"I know you are hurting, with all this incessant flirting.
I will now reveal someone, only for you I've kept in store."
To my doubting mind, she exclaimed, "Don't worry!
He will not bore."
      "I'll give a single peek, and nothing more."

With her arm around my shoulder, my eagerness
grew bolder. "Behind door one," directed
my guide, "is a man you will adore. A charming
salsa dancer whose physique is anything but crude."
I drank in this Apollo, yet I could not follow him to score.
Then, I conquered my will against this thrill and cast
him from my floor.
      For him, I'll swipe right, nevermore.

I reasoned and I wondered, is this quest a tragic blunder?
Did I embark on a sinful journey my parents would abhor?
"Mighty Aphrodite, I cannot continue blindly. Please show
me your directory, I implore, for this is a daunting chore."
"I see," she said. "No need to fret. Come this way,
let us explore.
      I bet you'll say, let's look no more."

Door number two flung open to a man who seemed soft spoken. In his moonlit chamber, this raven haired stranger, my faith controlled. He was unaware I was even there while consuming tales of ancient yore. At once, he saw me as from years before. "Oh my dear, I've missed you so," he crowed, "You are risen, my Lenor."
"For me he had a place, nevermore."

I left the chamber with no glee, full of spite for Aphrodite. I returned to find her smiling. Her demeanor beguiling. She said, for you, I have one more. Resigned, I threw caution to the wind. Though my patience had grown thin, I followed her through that third door. He appeared with an hourglass—the sand had just begun to pour.
Of him, I knew I wanted more.

"Hello," he said, "I'm here for you—when your profile came into view, I knew you would be unique, someone I could not ignore." There was much to understand. Before I could make demands, he said: "With you, time is never static, and our whole lives we can explore. You may show me all your faults, and yet still leave me wanting more.
My search continued, nevermore.

K2

Ransom Poem, June 4, 2012

MORNING son

A gem hidden in plain sight

Travel's
bag in his hands

Living TEN FEET FROM
himself and TIME

THE WORLD
IS NEVER ENOUGH

He IS
A Pioneer in
luster

Portland
2013

It's so green—

like okra
before it's
tossed into
tomato broth

I cross the bridge
of Multnomah Falls—

it roars
and sprays,
but I do
not flinch

Fog mists the
windshield
while driving
to PDX for an
early LA flight

I urge
him to run
the defroster

because
I can't
see—

He plays
video games
for hours
after studying
torts and

contracts
until dawn

I lock myself
in our room
because
he is not
a mind reader

I cry during
lunch at
Vita Cafe
about a
late ring

A doctor
examines
the rocks
in my head
and water
in my chest

The city feeds me
with injera

I walk my dog,
Happy,
under the
cerulean sky
on April 4th—
My grandmother
sends a warm
breeze to
embrace me

At the Japanese
garden, under
gray sky, he
slides a
kaleidoscope
on my finger

The roses have
just entered
their season

Glowing

PORTLAND, OR

December 16,

To Whom It May Concern:

The highest recommendation I can give is to Melineh Yemenidjian. The news of her departure to Southern California crushed our company because Melineh's work ethic is of the highest standard. Before her arrival, our store was very disorganized and the distribution of work was overloaded onto our sales staff which prohibited them from fully focusing on their primary tasks. This had been an ongoing problem until Melineh came to work for ███████. In a few short weeks, she had organized everything from our diamond inventory to our loan system. In addition to her organizational skills, Melineh is a self-starter and takes it upon herself to aid our staff in whatever needs to be done. No task is too small or big for her. She takes every duty very seriously and performs efficiently and professionally.

In addition to her stellar capabilities, Melineh is adored by our staff. Her positive and sunny disposition is infectious and well received by our customers. If you hire her you will be getting the finest gem.

If you don't, time to see a therapist.

If you have any questions or would like to speak further about Melineh, please do not hesitate to contact me.

Sincerely,

Owner and President

A Small Struggle

Death is a thief
a quick flutter in the dark
cleaving flesh from soul

Rift—
the abrupt letting go
of a granddaughter
2013

She, a soiled handkerchief
once kept proudly
in the pocket of your suit
is now boxed in a dingy
basement of forgotten
things: a can of soup
stocked in 1983, pajamas
wrapped in cellophane,
onyx lamps too
cumbersome to place
in the living room

She sits, this granddaughter,
3,000 miles away
wondering if you will
even attend her wedding

She knows the damage
has been done, she
did the unforgivable
of giving her virtue
before taking vows

She left her family's home
to make her own

Her convictions did not match yours

She did not bend—a flaccid daisy in the wind

You wanted to care for those
tender white petals your own way
but your green thumb
did not extend far enough
to provide nurture

There can be no shelters for daisies
for they grow in the wild
and need the warmth of sun—
the comfort of soft grass

They only last so long in vases—
you can't make them grow in glass

When she last saw you,
this granddaughter, she smiled and hugged
and kept silent
to suppress all the sadness
thumping inside of her chest—

Though not hardened
it became tough enough
to acknowledge
that you, born in 1924,
are set in your ways
and will never again
feel that levity
when squeezing orange juice
at 4 o'clock in the morning
or buying doughnuts
for your granddaughter
still cocooned on the couch

She now expects nothing
but wants everything,
and that makes her cry.

Never Lost
Ransom Poem

Memory,
A fold that stays in the mind

Memory,
THE OCEAN

memory,
a nation
of the
spirit world

Yed Sevi*

I remember

my country   stolen
                    I remember

heavy clouds.

                              quivering
                              barbar-

ous masters   I remember
                    the brink of abysses,

                              mingling with the

grave

and the metallic
Armenian   red

Yed Sevi translates to "back to black" in Armenian.

Care(less)

Care(less)
in HEAPing wisdom
Prop/aganda—a spider's web
belief in butter{fly}
when dung beetles roll
up the hill
Perp/pose in poll-ution
in an inst/ant
invaders crawl
into (mind)space-
and illustrate
tunnels leading
to free+dom(e)
ca-rv-ed by t[ears]

Krikor Shirozian
Syria, 1915

Dedicated to my great-grandfather
and all martyred in the Armenian Genocide

I never knew my name,
only Shiro, the town
ransacked by Turks.

They first arrested my father.
Then the rest of us. My mother
and I never saw him again.

We tumbled and limped to
the desert of Deir ez-Zor—
each step a searing agony.
Horse shoes were beaten
into the soles of those
who dared complain.

I woke one morning, my face
drenched with sweat.
I heard lowing sobs trapped
in our makeshift tent,
only to realize they were my own.

Hard ground had stolen the
warmth of my mother's lap.
Only her scarf remained,
draped over my brittle frame.

A hoarse "Mama" escaped my lips
as I clung to the thought that she might
be bartering for bread with the gold
sewn into the seams of her skirt.

Yet the caravan's supplies lay barren—
like the haunted darkness of Armenian eyes.

Suddenly, a man's silhouette loomed.
A pistol glared at me as his tongue
lashed like a whip.

A wet stain spread down
my tattered clothes. I covered
my face as the hammer clicked.
Before a single tear could fall,
the ground gave way.

Harsh wool grazed my skin
as sturdy arms hurled me over
the rippling muscles of a horse.

I awoke to the bustle of the Euphrates,
where a Kurdish family placed me in a wagon.

They spared my body but not my childhood
and were no better than the desert.

When asked for my name, I could not
tell them—from then on, I became Shirozian.

.

We, the Starving Angels

We, the starving angels
pinch stars
like mounds of salt
and sprinkle them
over barren soil,
expecting magic to sprout

Magic that breathes
like money
tucked in the pocket
of a well-tailored suit,
capable of replacing
life with litter

The root of our paralyzed souls
is forgotten—
this amnesia, a plague
perpetuated by muscle memory

We have learned to thrive in armor—
to build walls that can be seen
by our ancestors

There is no calm in our bellies—
we are the sea, swelling
with storm,
compelled to devour
anything good

Despite this,
we all seek solace
from a bite of bread
fresh out of the oven

Indisposed

I fit less with faith

This ashiest self
Is stifled, leash

And false thesis
Left see

Safe shift

Salt and slate

The life, a shelf

III.

"I take pleasure in my transformations,
I look quiet and consistent, but few know how
many women there are in me."

—Anais Nin

The Ant and the Crumb

Poetry is an ant
scavenging my brain
for a crumb
bigger than
itself—

But it will never
crumble under
the weight of...

"I don't know"

Pregnancy Cravings
Journal Entry, December 22, 2016

I am faced with the gnawing feeling
that my full potential is not met.
Is my barrier as a paid poet due to
lack of desire and laziness,
or is it simply not the right time?

There is no time like the present,
but I suppose my body and brain
can only support so much growth—
am I too hard on myself?

I should stop this torture
and enjoy my pregnancy.

—M.

The Meeting
Los Angeles, California, 2016

Our humble mission is carried forth
in a cluttered conference room
at end of day, when we still have
dinner to cook or taxes to tackle.

Red-rimmed eyes crackle in the pursuit
of justice. Opinions climb on top
of each other to address the
pressing issues of the day.

"The flyers are not mailed
  and the commemoration
  is in two weeks…"

"The elected officials have
  to be there,
  to hear our agenda,
  to be a part of the resolution!"

"We are still plagued by denial."

"The Armenian Genocide
  must be recognized!"

"1915 never again!"

Sadly, we are a small band
without a leader,
all too tired to work tirelessly.

The only ground covered:
"We will need two veggie platters."

Dejected, we file out of the smoke-stale room.
Nevertheless, electricity hums while the
lights wait to flicker back to life.

(De-vine)

One

ends

begins

and

the other

and is

sustains

all

Calla
April 9, 2017

the silent
         sorrow

    of a mother's
         wound/ed
            spirit   is   a
  single
       white
             lily~

    Ex{posed} and {delicate}

    in a universe forged
by the blaze

              of <birth>

Hello, Self

Hello, Self

I feel like I've lost you.
> That's ok. People lose things
> all the time. Usually,
> what's lost is right where
> they first looked—
> yet they are so
> frantic, it's missed.

I get what you're saying,
but it's hard to make the
connection.
> Keep looking. You may find
> other forgotten things along the way.
> Things that can be pleasant surprises.

Sure, but what do
surprises have to do
with losing myself?

> Nothing. Which is why you must
> maintain momentum while regarding
> the surprises as a nice break from
> beating yourself up.

Huh. Thank you, oh
Wise owl.
> Yes, you are. You know exactly what
> needs to be done. You're just not ready
> to do it. Take your time. Build your
> strength. Keep looking for your keys.

Doldrums

Journal Entry, October 14, 2019

"You've got to wake up every morning
With a smile on your face
And show the world all the love in your heart"
— *"Beautiful,"* by Carole King

There are days when all the synapses in my brain feel like they are rotting. I plaster a smile on my face, go to therapy, take pills to ease anxiety and stress, to sleep better—but all of this is temporary. It may trick my brain, but the real work is identifying the hungry creatures living beneath the surface. I have to sift through my life, like cleaning a hoarder's house, to find my truth. It hides behind the little lies, like wisps of the forest darting through trees, as if waiting for permission by a force greater than myself to come forth.

Frida Khalo said, "My painting carries with it the message of pain." I had a conversation with Chris about this, and he said most of the greats—like Frida, and a viscerally haunting poet, Edgar Allen Poe—wrote from despair and annihilation. I opposed it because tapping into the psyche's netherworld is terrifying. I wanted only happiness to inspire me, because writing about love as a hero eases the burden of neglect.

—M.

Mona
Journal Entry, November 18, 2019

"Friends don't vanish," I said aloud.
The air answered:
"Some friendships drift—
like sentences that forget their endings."
— The Phantom Tollbooth, by Norton Juster

Developing a kinship can feel like being whisked away past the tollbooth into a world of wonder. Such an adventure began with Ramona—Mona, as I called her—a kindred spirit from the very start.

We met in the City of Reality, where we recognized beauty and meaning in each other. Together, we reached toward the Castle in the Air, supporting one another through hardships and pain. In that process, we restored balance in our lives and, in doing so, discovered wisdom.

We relished in the whimsy of our unique creativity— she, an artist, and I, poet—wandering through a space like the Word Market. There, words are the currency, and we embraced the absurdity and wonder of making sense of the senseless, and vice versa.

The senselessness crept in around the time I gave birth to my son, and she to her daughter. Our world of jokes and stories morphed into silence, distance, and unanswered questions.

"I can't talk. I just can't," Mona told me during our last telephone conversation.

Her longtime boyfriend left her because he didn't see marriage and children in their near future. She attached herself to a man who idealized her in a way that left no room for who she really was. An accidental pregnancy crashed upon her—she ultimately fell prisoner to postpartum depression, and was placed on suicide watch by her doctor.

I tried to be there for her the best way I knew how. I suppose she thought the best way was no way—until we lost each other. I have tried to find her throughout the years, but since then I have resigned our escapades to memory."

–M.

Snack

Journal Entry, November 28, 2019

Eating a snack seems so vulnerable, as if hunger—without the formality of a sit-down meal— shows my naked humanity: a bite of a banana here, a power bar there, guzzling peanuts found at the bottom of my purse from my flight to Arizona two weeks ago. I was glad I found them, but needing them seemed desperate to me.

I felt sad, sitting alone in my car, tipping the cellophane bag in my hand, chewing the peanuts as quickly as possible to satisfy the monster gnawing at my stomach. I couldn't help it, even though I had a decent breakfast: two scrambled eggs and toast with jam.

I took my coffee to go in an insulated mug, because I refused the indignity of drinking it cold. I'd grown weary of hearing the sad splash of stale brown circling the drain because I hadn't given myself enough time to enjoy this comforting beverage.

—M.

Drinking a Cup of Black Coffee

Cue culpa
      Flee foe
Dig in bulk
      Grind; on coal
Fire
     Pour

          Relief

Chance

A line for life is all I need
to save me from my given lot

It is a story with no plot—
a protagonist with no heed

The race is run at breakneck speed,
a sensation of being free

Each chapter brings trials and strife,
but being a mother and wife
gives me reason to take care

And exit from under the snare
confronting fortuity rife

The Kiss

After Gustav Klimt's painting
of the same name, 1907–1908

He calls me **"Texas Mel"**
因为 because my dis-position
matches how quickly
we)ather change(s
it-self.

RIGHT NOW
a hurricane **!rages!**
through ridges
in my brain   and breaks
all the windows

Meanwhile, he cracks jokes
to keep the wind at bay

.

As glass
sHaTteRs
like dying fireflies,

I imagine:

:sunshine and wildflowers everywhere:
*
braided into a crown
*
woven through my dress
*
strewn upon the ground
*

~~~

Then the cold front

pushes through.

I sink
to my knees
and freeze

He places my hand
around his neck—
his breath warms my cheek.
My toes curl,

and his lips meet mine.

Quest

I didn't know where
to find it.

I searched
the cavity
in my chest,
and it was not
there.

I peeled back
my skull
and shook
the fleshy mass
embedded
so serenely—
it did not even stir.

I yelled,
red faced,
"Why are you
not doing your job!"

My cranky fingers
curled around
the hilt
of a hunting knife.

I gutted myself.
The whole thing
spilled silently
onto my feet
and the hydrochloric
acid ate it.

Then, whatever
still pulsed,
begged—

"Oh God..."

And all the jerk did
was smirk.

Then, whatever
still pulsed,
begged—

"Oh God..."

And all the jerk did
was smirk.

**why
do
i
bother?**

As I
lay
in
bed,
a
bull
comes
charging
through
the
ring
beyond
my
eyelashes,
and
fucks
it
all
up.

Crimson

Women are called
crazy, hysterical—
she-wolves, ready
to devour the
more logical,
reasonable sex

If prohibited,
our zest will meld
into bayonets
that will make
your nose and
mouth one*

*Inspired by the Armenian idiom, «Քիթդ ու բերանդ մէկ կ՚ընեմ:»
Which means, I will mess up your face.

Sweet Escape
Notepad Confessional

my sister rolls dough
too flat for a pizza

she pats it into a ball
again and sets it on
the marble countertop
dusted with flour

back and forth,
it expands
until just right

the sauce is spread, along
with freshly grated mozzarella
sprinkled along with olives,
bell peppers, tomatoes, and
onions. It goes into the oven
at 375 for twenty minutes

she settles on the couch, returns
to her embroidery and watches
a reality dating show,
until a burnt smell wafts
around the house

she had forgotten
to set the timer

the crust is blackened
and toppings burnt to a crisp

she trashes the remains

then light from the refrigerator
pools around her as she scans
the shelves and drawers

the door slams shut, and with a tub
of brownie batter ice cream under
her arm, my sister returns to her spot,
and presses play

All Here

There is too much grief here than this body will allow—
competition for hierarchy is based on levels of chaos.

Distraction is a flaming accident, an unavoidable Beauty;
viewed by the companion who rides shotgun next to Sorrow.

As sweet cherries paired at the stem dangling on Memory
dip into dreams, crickets play a violin's sinuous cradle.
The rocking chair of peace lulls my child to sleep in his
cradle. There is too much devotion here than this body
will allow—too much that will be lifted by "run past
my dress" Memory.

In all moments, the unbalanced books of life tumble in chaos,
once rested on foundations laid by hands who carry history's
Sorrow—a monument in ruins dedicated to Beauty.

The curse of the holy raising in prayer, is chased by Beauty.
Her prisms refract gnarled fingers looming above cradles,
as warm homes lie in the winter streets of Sorrow.

Bleak is the sentence for those birthed by a god not allowed.
They are strapped and carried toward the
salvation of chaos—
their lives scored like songs onto the rubble of Memory.

Dust clouds gather survivors and deliver them to Memory.
The struggle for grace is as jagged as a sca carved on Beauty—
a small reminder of how glory can seep out of chaos.

I sit in a fetal position, knees kissed and chin cradled.
Depression is injected as far as wallowing will allow,
the poison of loneliness stopped in time by Sorrow.

The giver of all poems and founder of freedom is Sorrow,
who strings secrets as a rope suspended over Memory.
Fear looks down, but has nowhere to go.

Space is demanded to allow long strides toward the
University of Beauty, where infinite life is naive and
will not be confined to cradles—though pleasure
may masquerade as wisdom and march with chaos.

The believer is convinced when justice rides on chaos.
Horses run fast past the carnage tended by Sorrow.
Faces are unwritten, and only one word hang on every cradle.

Serenity of pride is appeased in those with selective memory
who declare gardens unsanctified and shun their
frivolous beauty.

Yet plants and flowers thrive, because all here are all allowed.

Lady Libertine

No one has called me a libertine,
yet I think the title fits.
I want to live life, unrestrained,
often chomping at the bits

Moral tethers pull me close
to a life that is designed
to manage women in the throws
of passion, thriving in divine

I have a man and child
who depend on me at home,
but my spirit is without care
and wants to freely roam

I am pulled apart by mortal coil,
tossed by tempests of my past
to contrive meaning from the toil
and realign the cast

The North Star is my direction
when I sail too deep
but wanderlust roils in my bones
when tempted with delight

I Am Justice

I am imperfect
Imperfect cloud
Cloud before dusk
Dusk steeping horizon
Horizon too far
Far from me
Me, in solitude
Solitude is underrated
Underrated is normalcy
Normalcy brings sanity
Sanity is breaking
breaking past ego
Ego, the bond
Bond destroyer
Destroying friends
Friends who leave
Leave like seasons
Seasoning weather
Weather like moods
Mood of state
State of soul
States to travel
Travel wilderness
Wild cities
Cities like Portland
Portland becomes home
Home is Los Angeles
Los Angeles is not for angels
Angels unreachable
Unreachable dreams
Dreams give purpose
Purpose in life
Life turned to wife
Wife and mother
Mother and poet

Poet burrowing
Burrowing amid disaster
Disaster dictates
Dictates next step
Steps incur consequences
Consequences ripple
Ripple towards infinity
Infinity has no rules
Rules have no justice
Justice is relative

Twisted

Shadows pass
            without humming
                        nostalgia.

                Our lungs
            are bleeding
          accordions

while words
            whisper
                  the tango.

                I want us
              to be
            tonight—
          all day long.

Come back...

                  Hold me
              in our blue
            room.

Blind me,
            until
                  I can
                        see.

    Kill me,
                  so that I
              can rest—
          then kiss me
back to life.

Web

I weave
   a tapestry
      of shimmering silk
         to remind me
      how to care
         for what's mine—

      Then forget, as I link
         one line against
the other, dropping
     from plane to plane.

        The world is a blur
and the plunge, delicious.

Precarious

Careening
b(right and molasses
A sin-gle rod
straight
down
Releasing
it all
Safety evaporates
like sugar cane
Crystals
falling into tea
A s{l}ip
too soon
at[tack]s

The frenzied molecules need time
to orient around
sweetness

Poppy

my {mi}seedling{nd},
un-furl-s
      #carpe die^m
fee...ds
      ser?otonin

until   full bl∞m
          it   pushes
  from c r a c k s in a side=walk—

  fault lines
     mirro(ring/gnir)orrim a map—
  the compass a freshly
         d-r-a-w-n-> tar*get,

until the
rain of
April
falls

Awakening?

I think I hear god,
his angels, and the call
of the Universe—
I think I hear god.

Demons infiltrate my mind
as well. I try to protect
Myself against them—
Demons infiltrate my mind.

Like Mosquitos, they swarm
all around. The angels provide
no salvation from inhabitation—
Like Mosquitos, they swarm.

They feel real to me,
but I can't see.
Clearly, I have gone mad?
They feel real to me.

I think I hear the voice of god,
his angels, and the call
of the Universe—
I think I hear the voice of god.

Bipolar I Disorder, Mixed Episode
February 2020

Hy[ersex-usual
Para/no-ise-a
psycho-sister
Oversocial
can't stop thinking
not real-eyes-ing
that this is no
spiritual
away/kin-ing

Reality
dropped dead
head explo(re)ded
life became
a casual-tea
ripped lace
disgraced—
sudden
stammer,
raised
hammer,
endless
clamour

It boil/spoil-ed over
a cra(ked egg
in an angry pot
the whites oo*zZz*ed
out like brain
matter—no.thing
mattered—felt
nothing

Then a hush
gripped my elbow—
slowed tornado
tethered my wild,
moored into mild

I hugged back
cut me some slack
cried a river
sweated, shivered

Burned some bridges
railed some ridges
recovered my senses
doled recompenses

Now, a beat-up
car, not broken
or whole—
engine's running
on empty
so I'm on foot,
to find my roots—
mile after mile
smile after smile

Equ-I-Pose

I WALLOW
between |wedged| stone

little

do I k(now)

the more I c{rumble},

the c.lose.r   **< I Am>**

to

Ev-()-lution.

122

Admitted

Journal Entry, March 18, 2020
Written from a Kaiser Permanente outpatient facility
during a 72-hour psychiatric hold

I checked myself into the emergency room on March 17, 2020. I had begun writing a suicide letter to my husband, half believing the world would be better off without me.

I thought it was no big deal, that my brain was making things up or being melodramatic, but then, words like that don't materialize from nowhere. Last time my brain turned suicidal and desperate, I began reaching out to strangers to ease my loneliness and perceived isolation. Not only was this approach misguided, it was also coupled with undiagnosed Bipolar I Disorder with Mixed Features.

Unbeknownst to me, people with my condition have a predisposition for addiction, hypersexualization, delusions such as hearing, seeing, and feeling things that aren't there—I have experienced all of them. In a day, I could go from a 0 to a 10 on the mood scale. I also believed that I was the reincarnation of Eve and the Virgin Mary and my mission on Earth was to heal all of mankind. This lasted until Chris confronted me about my questionable behavior.

Since my admission, I have been by myself, except for the nurse who comes in a few times a day to check my vitals and to provide me with essentials like food, change of clothes, and medication. I was seen by the psychiatrist for five minutes within hours of my admission—I haven't seen another, or a therapist since. I'm also quarantined because of a miscommunication. They thought I had been exposed to COVID-19, which I wasn't, so I have to stay here anywhere from 2 to 5 days until I get the all clear, which means my care is to be delayed and who knows when they will be able to find me a bed at in-patient.

—M.

Self-Deliverance

In this antiseptic
arena of eternal
phosphorescence

Angels crawl,
scraping linoleum,

and their counterparts
float on clouds

while I, shrouded
in green paper,
am strapped
to a bed.

No amount of
prayer or pills shoved
in my mouth
could ease this
malevolent rapture—

Only I can save myself.

Mood Monitor

Journal Entry, March 19, 2020
Written from a Kaiser Permanente outpatient facility
during a 72-hour psychiatric hold

2:00 pm

Today around 7:30 a.m., they switched my room, and for a few hours, I could not locate my flip-phone or my books. A panic attack on top of anxiety soon followed, but I did not receive any attention or care from my nurse, which led to a deep feeling of isolation and suicidal ideation. I was really low until I went through my yoga vinyasa and then balanced my chakras through meditation. The distraction soothed my mind.

I eventually found my phone and called Chris, who has been my rock and advocate through this ordeal. Without his help, I don't believe I would be able to stay in a consistent mental state, at least not without maximum effort. I cycled through anxiety and emptiness a few times until I finally received my medication and a fresh change of hospital-issued paper scrubs around noon—hours after my request. Had it not been for Chris, who also brought my laptop, I probably wouldn't have gotten what I needed until my overworked nurse returned to check my vitals again.

About 45 minutes after my dose of Lamictal, I felt a rush of energy. It was short-lived, but I maintained it through yoga.

Chris called moments ago to say hello with Norayr, and I got weepy because I missed them, and being here without them is harder than I thought it would be. Other than that, I feel nothing.

I'm watching *It's Kind of a Funny Story* for the third time. I chose this movie due to my impending visit to an inpatient psych ward. It comforts me to know that my future experience won't be frightening, but an opportunity to grow out of my cycle of self-sabotage. My mood lifted after Craig sang *Under Pressure* by David Bowie and Queen (a favorite band). A very appropriate song for my time in the ER.

7:50 pm

There is a familiar tingling in my head and my energy is low again. I think my mental state is balanced enough. I told Dr. D, my primary psychologist, about my admittance and what I wanted to say to the inpatient once I go there:

"I'm here because I need immediate help managing balance with my bipolar symptoms. My current medication is not at the recommended dose, but will be next week. I have suicidal ideations and see and hear things that aren't there when I least expect it. It is not uncommon for me to experience depression and mania at the same time, which can range from unsettling to frightening. I also feel disconnected from the people in my life and the activities that once brought me joy. I find it hard to move from the couch in my lowest times, and in my mania, I've reached a drastic psychosis during which I have no sense of reality. I want help to achieve equilibrium. Even though I have had ongoing therapy and sporadic psychiatric care, I feel it has been inadequate in helping me cope with and manage my symptoms."

"To whom much has been given, much
will be required."
—Luke 12:48

I have been blessed with so much. I know that sounds
like a cliché, but it is true. There is a lot I have had to
overcome to get to this point, and still more ahead. God
has asked a lot of me because the way ahead cannot be
easy, and He wants to know that I can hack it. Parts
of moving forward can be wonderful, and other parts
drive me to the point of wanting to give it all up. The
important thing is that I didn't, and I'm seeking help—
the help I need to find balance, then joy and, finally,
appreciation of myself.

9:38 pm

My parents are in denial over the severity of my con-
dition. They believe exhaustion is the root. They think
that if I just get some rest, meditate, or do yoga, I can
push past it, even though I've been telling them for two
years that something is wrong with me. Now, I have
a clinical reason. Perhaps after some kind of medi-
ated group session to share my truth, we can rebuild
our relationship.

What makes me the most frustrated is that even though
they are supportive, they don't know what they are sup-
porting. I've tried to tell them, but they brush it off be-
cause they don't understand mental illness. They think
if I stay positive, do yoga, and meditate, all my prob-
lems will be cured. But my problems are problems be-
cause of the way my brain reacts to different situations.

March 20, 2020

5:15 am

Thank God. My new nurse is Brenda. She has been my best nurse—kind, attentive, cooperative, and compassionate. Unlike April, my nurse from yesterday, who delayed my nightly dose of trazodone. I requested it at 9:30 pm but didn't get it until 11:30. After I had a severe anxiety attack, I filtered through all my coping mechanisms for about 30 minutes until the security guard saw me in distress and told them I needed attention urgently.

—M.

Note: After all this, I found out that Kaiser does not provide inpatient psychiatric services.

In the Shadow of Grace
Inspired by the Ghazal

Pain is raked across my soul,
rumination taking toll

I judge the faults dealt by others
which in myself I've lost control

Unable to see through my tears
these fears have dug me in a hole

Too proud to extend my shaking hand,
I am down this rising well alone

Above, the sky is painted gray
like my numbing mood, forlorn

I thrash and claw to find my way, but
the cold has chilled me to the bone

The quiet here is so loud
and heavy as a rolling stone

My body is tired and grows limp
I sink cross-legged upon my throne

For I have exiled myself
to this state all on my own

Underwater, I open my eyes
and see everything I've ever known

My dreams and kin are floating here
as illusions only loaned

My heart begins to ache and swell
with care I've reaped and surely shone

This space is growing darker now—
like my spirit, no longer sound

Please, I do not want leave this world
having lived but not gone 'round

I must climb out without a rope
and learn from every slip and groan

This suffering and pain inflicted
sheds the self I will not mourn

I wear it as a cape along with
courage weaved with garnered scorn

The lip is near and may as well
be a vast and distant shore

Yet hope, like fingertips, spreads
and whispers: "Unfurl your wings and soar."

IV.

"The secret of joy
is in the mastery of pain."

—Anais Nin

List-
ening
Notepad Confessional

List-
ening
is an
egg
stuck
in my
throat
as I
cons-
trict
my
mus-
cles
to swal-
low.

Anna
Journal Entry, July 26, 2021

10:56 am

Good morning,

Some mornings are not good. Either I have trouble getting up (but have to anyway because… Norayr), or there are mornings like today, when the night before was sore. I had a psychotic episode and auditory hallucinations, so I took a medication prescribed for the first time by my psychiatrist to help with, and I quote, "odd voices—"quetiapine.

6:13 pm

Hello,

Today is an exceptionally uncomfortable day. The quetiapine side effects still have their hold, as does irritability, and the sensation of crawling out of my skin.

8:05 pm

Things got bad really quickly, but I remained in control the whole time. I cried for release, took two Ativan for relief, meditated for peace, then called the Kaiser helpline for wisdom. The crisis counselor Anna suggested I take a shower and listen to music, which I did. Norah Jones's 2002 album Don't Know Why popped into my mind—the lyrics from the song "Feeling the Same Way" about dealing with battling mental illness and the consequences of not "finding one's head."

My hope for this journal is to chronicle, in real time, the timeline, characteristics, intensity, moods, and outcome of my episodes and flare-ups.

I want to demystify bipolar. Get it down to my level and understand it as if it is a real person. Then, through the work, integrate and treat each other with tenderness and kindness. Most of all, we have to listen to each other.

I will name my bipolar alter ego Anna, after the kind and tender woman who helped me remember that I need to slow down and not push myself so hard.

—M.

Nene
Journal Entry, August 31, 2021

Dear Anna,

I'm staying at my parents' house tonight and found old photographs of my grandmother, Armenouhi, my father's mother. One of them captures my memory of her—vibrant, her head full of dark hair—the beautiful matriarch who raised five boys in poverty. She later referred to raising her seven granddaughters in America as a "luxury."

Another picture showed her thinner, wearing a navy turban, her skin pale where her eyebrows should have been. However, despite the cancer ravaging her body, her smile remained radiant.

She appears in my dreams once in a while or embraces me through the wind. It stirs up so much emotion that, when I see her face printed on this priceless paper, tears fall hotly around my eyes.

My memories of her are fading—yet the way she protected, pampered, and revered me will remain like a hand-knitted shawl over my shoulders.

—M.

Therapy

Lately,
          my mind
   has been a

Bumble Bee.

     Instead
               of making
Honey,   however,

          it forages
             seventy percent of

my Weight
          in tar.

     Tar so viscous
that

     when it fills
my stomach
          I plummet
like a hive
     filled with beetles.

          To keep
flying, I engage in

     trophallaxis
               in hopes   the
Worker bee
          can metabolize
this

     sludge
               to
Sugar

So that I may,
yet again,

mind my own
Beeswax.

To Chris:
Your superfluously
simple tongue
is my favorite thing
about you

My husband emits
a loud, rude noise
when I begin to speak.

He is watching football
on the recliner, eating
Doritos out of the bag.

I know that when he is
facing the TV on Sundays
he is at church, and the only
thing he hears is the booming
sermon of the commentator—
the preacher from the pulpit
in the sky.

I, however, am sacrilegious
and have a more pressing
issue to discuss—

The downward spiral of
my mental state.

"Chris," I say,
rubbing my temples.

"I'm having another
episode."

"Motherfucking piece of shit
cocksucking whore!" He yells.

A football guy
gets tackled and
suffers a concussion.

"Chris!"

"Did you see that?! There goes
my fantasy football season,"
he groans as if he feels the
injured player's pain.

Amid the cacophony circling my brain,
I have an idea:

"Want to hear my fantasy?" I say.

His head whips my way.

"What are we talking about?
Bondage, professor-student,
or dungeon master and prisoner?"

"No. A husband who wants to listen
to how my world is plunging into
the abyss."

"There is no listening in my fantasies,
unless it's to commands," he says,
eyes glinting with mischief.

"Babe,
you can't fuck away depression."

"Sure you can. The release
causes endorphins to flood
your brain, thus freeing you from
the grips of despair."

"I see. Well,
the only thing flooding me
right now is the need
to throw my shoe at the TV."

"Why would you do such a thing?"

"Because you're trying
to distract me so I can feel
better."

He shrugs.

"Isn't that what I'm supposed to do?"

Personal Legend
Journal Entry, July 31, 2021
After The Alchemist by Paolo Coelho

7:12 am

Anna,

A poem flew out of my brain today. I suppose my creative synapses have begun firing again in unison. I have to thank you for that—you and this episode, if it's still living in my body. It hasn't shown itself since Wednesday, and even then, only briefly.

I know I'm destined to do great things and have subconsciously been preparing for it. Yet life's work requires living life.

In October 2019, I asked the universe to send me a sign. I was tired of the nameless churning, like cogs grinding inside me—or like flint striking rock, creating sparks of what I believed was genius. Either way, I needed a major upset in my life to feel whole.

When I write, I hear a voice—it's more of a feeling translated into words. Sometimes it's kind and thoughtful, like now. Other times, it's harsh and cruel, even demonic. Additionally, there is a part of me that lives in fantasy, which is the most dangerous—though I haven't heard it since February 2020, when I was first diagnosed.

For months, however, I was tangled in mania and depression, delusions of grandeur, and worthlessness—all at the same time.

Even though I still experience the painful shifts of bipolar, my awareness of symptoms and learned coping strategies make life bearable.

—M.

On Shaming

After "On Loving" by Forugh Farrokhzad

Tonight, from prying eyes,
razors descend upon this poem.
My mind struggles to survive
the betrayal of my hand.

My virginal, naive poem,
dictated by its desires,
follows a string of ignorant men
with restless, greedy fingers.

Yes, so shame begins
on the road not known but learned.
It is not on any map, for there
is no treasure to be earned.

Why shun beauty?
A rose dragged by the stem
is no less a rose when plucked
of its petals and shorn of thorns.

Let me lose myself here,
on this page—let sage
wisdom lead my courage
like wildflowers picked at dusk.

I do not wish to be wrapped
like an invalid or child—I have
fought too hard and too long
to let my resolve grow mild.

Do you know what I want in life?
For this poem to roost then travel
like a raven searching for secrets—
never satisfied for too long.

Concealed in my poem is a grave
of memories that have grown stale—
they no longer have the power to
lacerate my hope and blind my will.

I am no longer filled with shame.
The ink in my thoughts, black as sin,
now etched in my skin, tells
the story that pulses within.

I am no longer filled with shame.
I do not bury my head in the crook
of my arm when I think of the times
I have fallen from grace.

Yes, so shame ends
on the road not known but learned.
It is not on any map, for there is
no treasure to be earned.

Hang Time
March 2025
After my favorite ride at Knott's Berry Farm
and a tête-à-tête with fellow poet Joseph Bravo

To discourse with
            a (fell)ow Poe/t
is to s—end   you   on   a
                              roller
                              coaster

  You sit together,
  |Knees)(touching|

        S*miles are compulsory
                because
        you know
                what's coming,
          and yet...
                you don't

      The horizon is straight ahead
                        but you won't rip through it
      like a (ban)ner at a football game

            upward
It will inch   to   threaten
                  heave/n.

      The car
            lurches
                  at the peak
                        and dangles
            long enough   to span

the bustling
World.

Each dip
captures breath
long enough
to hear Madness
Taunting
Gravʒity

The car abstains from
the   track
  far enough to keep sparks

from   flying!

Hands shoot
resistant
against

Wind's
  weight—

        grasping for any   bit
    of sky as   Keepsake
    for the thrill of

hurtling
  {the mind}

muses combust—

Screams raise in concert
and trav-
el like streamers

The color of

  ~peacock feathers~

The Genesis of a Poem

You, like the matron of a bordello,
seduce me. You fill coins of gold
in my mouth left on chests by regulars
who cultivate tête-à-têtes
like the Bible swallows myths.

Your hand is a stone that sends
ripples along my arm, leading me
down a candle lit hallway.
Keys on the ring clink together when
you lock my room after I step inside.

Stripped—I, a woman
tattooed with roads of stretch marks
and a cesarean scar like the portal
of a valley sliced by a craggy river.

I lie waiting on a lace spread.
The boudoir is scented with rose and musk—
the furniture draped in soiled silk.

Sweat competes for a place
on my skin against the albatross
studded with emeralds
clasped around my neck.

The burden is my penance for
slipping away to this secret place
where I can buck with abandon

and at once become virginal—

a neat plot of soft, green grass
ready to be strewn with seeds.
The lock clicks and my pulse
flurries like a scribbling hand.

A figure cracks the door and
stumbles in. It is my friend, who
has become a ghost.

Her long, blond hair is now cut short.
Her eyes, like cracked lenses, project
distorted reels of our long-lost sisterhood
and what would have been if she wasn't so
broken. Then she flickers away, a hologram.

Through the door, in a burst of light
appears a string of ex-lovers, a psychiatrist,
my husband pushing our children in a
red wheelbarrow, grandmothers holding
pomegranates, bullies, and my poetic ancestors—
arm in arm.

They gather around my bed and stare.
Then you, dark dahlia, part the crowd,
slide yourself through my fingers, and bleed
as I pluck your petals.

Acknowledgments

Since the age of twelve when I sought friendship in books, my goal has been to write my own. Poetry is the vessel that has brought others who seek kinship to journey with me. I thank the phenomenal people below for helping me catch and release my dream:

Christopher, my husband and a source of unconditional support.

Tommy Domino, my instructor for the Community Literature Initiative (CLI) Long Beach Chapter, who facilitated the frequency that my pen met paper.

Hiram Simms, founder of CLI, for his vision and conviction that every poet should have the opportunity to create their own books.

My father and mother, Noubar and Maggie Merdjanian, who knew from the beginning that poetry would be my destiny. They did everything possible to encourage the development of my poetic skill and talent.

A heartfelt credit to those who created the artwork for this book:

Front Cover, Norayr Yemenidjian
Author Picture, D. Hideo Maruyama

Finally, I thank the following publications for showcasing my work over the years:

"Tea," first published in VoiceCatcher, Winter 2015

"Equ-I-Pose," "Lady Libertine," "How to Trap a Butterfly," "Religion at Armenian School" first published in h-pem, 2020

"Without Bounds," first published in HyeBred Magazine, Winter 2024

"Iridescence," first published in volume 2 of Noor literary magazine, February 2025

"On Shaming," first published in Hey Young Writer, March 2025

"Poems," first published in Hey Young Writer, April 2025

"The Genesis of a Poem," "Concealed, 1970," and "Krikor Shirozian," first published in volume 2 of Jewel City Review, May 2025

Publisher's Note

The mission of Daxson Publishing is to bridge the disparity between mainstream literature and underserved voices. Our services are designed to remove typical obstacles wedged against those who are ready to publish their work. The Daxson team will treat your manuscript with the attention and respect it deserves.

Please submit at daxsonpublishing@gmail.com.

Your story will be in good company! To learn more about us and our artists, visit daxsonpublishing.com and provide support by purchasing books.

www.ingramcontent.com/pod-product-compliance
Lightning Source LLC
Chambersburg PA
CBHW021153130626
46554CB00005B/1803